WHY
GOD'S WORD
IS ALL
WE NEED

TODAY'S
ISSUES

WHY

GOD'S WORD

IS ALL

WE NEED

GENE
EDWARD
VEITH

CROSSWAY BOOKS • WHEATON, ILLINOIS
A DIVISION OF GOOD NEWS PUBLISHERS

Why God's Word Is All We Need

Copyright © 2000 by the Alliance of Confessing
Evangelicals

Published by Crossway Books
a division of Good News Publishers
1300 Crescent Street
Wheaton, Illinois 60187

First printing, 2000

Printed in the United States of America

ISBN 1-58134-168-7

The Alliance of Confessing Evangelicals exists to call the
church, amidst our dying culture, to repent of its worldli-
ness, to recover and confess the truth of God's Word as
did the Reformers, and to see that truth embodied in doctrine, worship and life.

Library of Congress Cataloging-in-Publication Data
Veith, Gene Edward, 1951-
   Why God's Word is all we need / Gene Edward Veith.
      p.   cm. — (Today's issues)
   Includes bibliographical references.
   ISBN 1-58134-168-7 (trade pbk. : alk. paper)
   1. Bible—Evidences, authority, etc. 2. Bible—Theology. 3. Word of
God (Theology) I. Title. II. Today's issues (Wheaton, Ill.)
BS480.V37 2000
220.1—dc21   99-045157
                                                          CIP

15	14	13	12	11	10	09	08	07	06	05	04	03	02	01	00
15	14	13	12	11	10	9	8	7	6	5	4	3	2	1

CONTENTS

PREFACE

These are not good days for the evangelical church, and anyone who steps back from what is going on for a moment to try to evaluate our life and times will understand that.

In the last few years a number of important books have been published, all trying to understand what is happening, and they are saying much the same thing even though the authors come from fairly different backgrounds and are doing different work. One is by David F. Wells, a theology professor at Gordon-Conwell Theological Seminary in Massachusetts. It is called *No Place for Truth*. A second is by Michael Scott Horton, vice president of the Alliance of Confessing Evangelicals. His book is called *Power Religion*. The third is by the well-known pastor of Grace Community Church in California, John F. MacArthur. It is called *Ashamed of the Gospel*. Each of these authors is writing about the evangelical church, not the liberal church, and a person can get an idea of what each is saying from the titles alone.

Yet the subtitles are even more revealing. The subtitle of Wells's book reads *Or Whatever Happened to Evangelical Theology?* The subtitle of Horton's book is *The Selling Out of the Evangelical Church*. The subtitle of John MacArthur's work proclaims, *When the Church Becomes Like the World*.

When you put these together, you realize that these careful observers of the current church scene perceive that today evangelicalism is seriously off base because it has abandoned its evangelical truth-heritage. The thesis of David Wells's book is that the evangelical church is either dead or dying as a significant religious force because it has forgotten what it stands for. Instead of trying to do God's work in God's way, it is trying to build a prosperous earthly kingdom with secular tools. Thus, in spite of our apparent success we have been "living in a fool's paradise," Wells declared in an address to the National Association of Evangelicals in 1995.

John H. Armstrong, a founding member of the Alliance of Confessing Evangelicals, has edited a volume titled *The Coming Evangelical Crisis*. When he was asked not long afterwards whether he thought the crisis was still coming or is actually here, he admitted that in his judgment the crisis is already upon us.

The Alliance of Confessing Evangelicals is addressing this problem through seminars and conferences, radio programs, *modern* REFORMATION magazine, Reformation Societies, and scholarly writings. The series of booklets on today's issues is a further effort along these same lines. If you are troubled by the state of today's church and are helped by these booklets, we invite you to contact the Alliance at 1716 Spruce Street, Philadelphia, PA 19103. You can also phone us at 215-546-3696 or visit the Alliance at our website: www.AllianceNet. org. We would like to work with you under God "for a modern Reformation."

James Montgomery Boice
President, Alliance of Confessing Evangelicals
Series Editor, Today's Issues

ONE

How God Communicates with Us

A friend of mine tells about a young woman she knew who had mistreated her parents, spurning their love and writing them out of her life. Later she became a Christian. But even after her conversion, she still never bothered to reconcile with her mother and father. My friend finally asked her about it. "I will," said the young woman, "when the Lord tells me to." As of yet, she explained, the Lord hadn't urged on her heart that she should make up with her parents. She was willing to do so, but only if God wanted her to do it. And if he did, she expected that God would make his will clear to her through the Holy Spirit.

"Do you want to know what God wants you to do about your parents?" asked my friend. "You don't need to wait for him to tell you his will. Let's see what he says about it." She opened a Bible to Exodus 20:12. "Honor your father and your mother," she read. "That's what God tells you to do," she explained. "That's God making his will clear to you through the Holy Spirit."

That exchange points out two completely different ways of relating to God. Many people expect God to inspire them directly. They cultivate a God within who gives them the right emotions, puts ideas into their heads, and communicates to them in a sort of nonverbal ESP.

Others believe God has revealed himself objectively—not in inchoate feelings or impressions but in human language. They do not look inside themselves to know God; rather, they look to his Word. They believe that God's will, what he has done for us, and his personal involvement in our lives are expressed in a unique, inspired, supernatural book—one that is on nearly everyone's shelves, making God accessible whenever someone wants to open its pages—a book known as the Holy Bible.

All Christians express some sort of allegiance to the Bible. But many Christians are uneasy about the Reformation insistence on *sola Scriptura,* "Scripture alone," the notion that the Word of God is sufficient for us, the only revelation we actually need. The result is that many try to supplement the Bible with human reason, scientific scholarship, sociological research, or the findings of modern psychology. Still others try to supplement the Bible with mystical experiences, inner convictions, and personal revelations. We see a great deal of this in Christian circles today.

I understand that. What I cannot understand is Christians who maintain that subjective revelations offer a more personal and intimate relationship with God than is afforded by the Bible. I say this because a true personal relationship with God— that is, a genuine, person-to-Person interaction—is only possible through the means of language.

Language is the means by which human beings both communicate and commune with each other. To have a relationship with another human being involves talking to that person and listening to what the other person has to say. There can be no personal relationships without communication of some kind. Merely basking in each other's presence is not enough. Merely feeling strongly or having strong affection for the other person is not enough. A couple has to talk with each other; not one or the other, but both partners have to talk or the relationship will die.

Language is the means we have of conveying our thoughts, our feelings, and our very selves to someone else. Language imparts information, but it does more than that—it is the only way we have of getting to know another person. It is through language that we connect with another human being. Even small talk keeps the connection going. Without language we would be essentially alone.

Linguists point out how language is fundamental to nearly every human activity. Thought depends on language. Cultures consist of people who speak the same language, and that language binds, defines, and shapes the community. Law and science, governments and the media, the great ideas and the way we entertain ourselves—it all consists of words, words, words. In fact, in a sense what sets human beings apart from animals is the capacity for language.

Furthermore, the capacity for language is part of what it means to have been made in the image of God. From the very beginning God is described as someone who speaks. God's creation was accomplished when he spoke: "And God said, 'Let there be light, and there was light.' . . . And God said, 'Let there be an expanse between the waters. . . .' And God said, 'Let the water under the sky be gathered to one place, and let dry ground appear.' . . . Then God said, 'Let the land produce vegetation.' . . . And God said, 'Let there be lights in the expanse of the sky.' . . . And God said, 'Let the water teem with living creatures.' . . . And God said, 'Let the land produce living creatures.' . . . Then God said, 'Let us make man in our image, in our likeness'" (Gen. 1:1-26). Thus the universe itself was spoken into being.

God is no mere object but a Person—and in the mystery of the Trinity a relationship of Persons—who in an incomprehensibly transcendent way thinks, feels, reflects, and communicates. Moreover, just as one cannot separate one's language from oneself, God's Word—his language—is his identity. "In the beginning was the Word, and the Word was with God, and the Word was God. He was with God in the beginning. Through him all things were made; without him nothing was made that has been made" (John 1:1-3). Then we learn that this Word is none other than Jesus Christ, the second Person of the Trinity: "The Word became flesh and lived for a while among us" (v. 14).

God is a Person, and he made human beings to be persons also, which includes the capacity for language. As soon as Adam was created, God reflected that this human being needed relationships. "The LORD God said, 'It is not good for the man to be alone'" (Gen. 2:18). So he gave Adam the linguistic task of naming, first the animals (2:19-20) and then the woman he loved (2:23; 3:20).

Why should we be surprised that God speaks to his children in actual, concrete, verbal, readable language? God is so far beyond us, how could we know anything about him unless he chose to take the initiative and reveal himself to us? Would we expect this revelation to be mere feelings? Don't we need more than that, actual knowledge about God, how he considers us and what he has done to restore our relationship? What better way could be conceived than that God should address us through language, that he should give us his Word?

This Word, if it is to be of any benefit to us mortals, must be in human language. How the Persons of the Godhead communicate with each other, what form God's Word assumed when he spoke the universe into existence, will be intrinsically unfathomable to the fallen, radically limited human mind. If God, in his amazing grace, deigns to communicate with us, it must be in terms we can understand. His language must be the language of actual human beings, historically and culturally situated, as all human language is, with grammar and syntax and vocabulary, capable of being translated and written down. God, as is his wont, works through means: "Holy men of God spoke as they were moved by the Holy Spirit," wrote Peter (2 Pet. 1:21, NKJV). What they spoke was recorded. Christ's apostles wrote down his Word. Indeed, "All Scripture is God-breathed" (2 Tim. 3:16).

Human relationships depend on communication in language, and this is also true of a relationship with God. Christians speak to God in prayer. God speaks to Christians in the words of the Bible.

People often say, "Show me God" or "If I could only see God, then I could believe." Many religions are based on visions. But for the people of the Bible, a god that one can see is not the true God. The pagan neighbors of the children of Israel had gods they could see. The sun that one can see in the sky every morning was a god; so were the stars, the sea—indeed, every quality of nature. Moreover, their gods were visible as carved images, adored in their homes and temples. The God of Abraham and Isaac, on the other hand, was most emphatically not even to be represented in visual terms. He was to be known only in terms of his Word.

The Bible says little about "seeing" God, but it says a great deal about "hearing" him. To be sure, after death we shall see God (1 Cor. 13:12). But for now, we must *listen* to him, and what we must listen to is the Bible.

TWO

Meeting God in the Bible

I remember when I first began to read the Bible seriously. I had read theologians from Lewis to Tillich, but I had never read the Bible, except in little snippets. I resolved to read the whole thing from beginning to end, an enterprise that took me from the beginning of the universe to the end of time—from Genesis to Revelation. I suppose I began my Bible-reading project for literary reasons, but as I read I found that I was meeting God.

A Personal Narrative

From the outset I was drawn in by the majestic narratives of Genesis and Exodus. Parts of them—the creation, the Fall, the saga of Joseph, the redemption of the Israelites out of slavery—were unutterably sublime. Other parts—God's seeking to kill Moses, hardening Pharaoh's heart, insisting on elaborate ceremonies and bloody sacrifices—were charged with mystery.

By the time I got to the Promised Land along with the children of Israel, I was reading about whole people being put under the ban and totally slaughtered—men, women, children, even animals—all wiped out by the command of God. This was shattering. God's people were given the Promised Land, but first Joshua had to take it forcefully and wipe out the existing inhabitants. This didn't seem fair to the Canaanites, as bad as they no doubt were. It seemed so barbaric, so extreme. I had assumed God was . . . well, nice.

These troubling passages were nevertheless consistent with the sublimity and mystery I was finding in the Bible. I could not dismiss them or explain them away. The God I was reading about was indeed righteous, as the human beings I was reading about—including the famous heroes of the faith—most emphatically were not. As I was reading about God's fury, I realized that his righteousness is infinitely above me and that—can I say it?—there is a danger in God.

Specifically, I realized that God is far, far different from me. He is "other." I realized that until then my idea of God had consisted of qualities that I liked. He was loving, kind, and tolerant, beaming down on us all, but not demanding too much; he was there when I needed him, but not too intrusive. The God that emerged as I read the Bible was far more intractable, far more complex. He was real. I understood that my theology consisted mostly of a smorgasbord of wish fulfillments. I had been picking out religious concepts that appealed to me. But nothing that is actually real merely conforms to our personal preferences. Reality can be known only by its hard edges. How could a real religion, one that is objectively, transcendently true, be grounded in my own desires?

As I kept reading, I realized that I had been trying to create a god in my own image, rather than the other way around. I had been creating my own god, pretty much like the apostate Israelites and doomed Canaanites had been doing with their handmade idols. At this point it hit me that God's ban—his merciless destruction of the people of the land that I found deeply shocking—applied to me.

I was reading desperately now. By this time I was in Judges, and I noticed a recurrent pattern.

God's people, despite everything he had done for them, lapsed into sin and idolatry and their consequences. God then sent leaders to save them—Moses, Gideon, and the other judges. Then I understood all those chapters about the tabernacle and why the Bible put so much emphasis on blood sacrifices. Why the blood of the lamb saved the slaves from the angel of death. Why the elaborate sacrificial system was necessary. Why on the Day of Atonement the high priest poured the blood of the sacrifice over the Ark of the Covenant so that the blood covered the broken tablets of the Law.

I modified my Bible reading plan at this point and began reading parts of the New Testament along with the Old. Not that there was a difference in the message—both spoke to me of Christ.

I knew myself as a cursed and condemned sinner whose condition before this transcendent and holy God was far worse than I could have dreamed in my worst nightmare. But I discovered that salvation is a free gift, not of my own doing but a matter of this transcendent God's inexplicable grace, won by the life, death, and resurrection of his Son and, mysteriously, credited to me. As I read the accounts of the life and teachings of Christ and the Pauline epistles, the message of the Bible came together, and I believed it. What began as a literary exercise ended in life-transforming faith.

I now understand what was happening to me in that little Bible reading project, and I have the vocabulary to describe it. I was confronted with God's Law, which brought me into a state of repentance. At that point I became receptive to the Gospel, the good news of forgiveness in Jesus Christ. God's Word was convicting me both of my sin and of his great grace.

The Bible conveys a great deal of information—true, reliable, authoritative information about God, history, theology, and how we should live. But we must remember that God's revelation is more than information. He reveals not only facts about himself—he reveals himself. His Word acts in a personal way upon the hearts of those who hear or read it. As the Reformers put it, God's Word is a means of grace.

If the Bible were mere information, a person who knows biblical doctrine backwards and forwards would no longer need the Bible. But the fact is, the most learned theologians and the most pious believers read the Bible all the more. Nor is the reading done once one has become a Christian. In my case, reading the Bible brought me from liberal theology to biblical faith. Yet I return to God's Word constantly since it keeps bringing me to repentance and to Christ. It is how I grow in the Christian life.

Reading the Bible keeps us personally connected to God.

The Power of God's Word

The power of God's Word was evident when he spoke the universe into existence out of nothing. But similarly, God can and does speak life into the nothingness of a sinful heart.

The Bible gives testimony to its own power: "The word of God is living and active. Sharper than any double-edged sword, it penetrates even to dividing soul and spirit, joints and marrow; it judges the thoughts and attitudes of the heart" (Heb. 4:12). The Word of God is not inert marks on paper; it is alive. It is active, working in people's lives. This text also highlights its "cutting" power, its ability to cut through our facades and defenses, killing in us what needs to be killed. Thus the Word is often symbolized as a sword, as in the injunction to take "the sword of the Spirit, which is the word of God" (Eph. 6:17). A particularly revealing example is in the book of Revelation, which several times depicts the risen and exalted Christ as one "out of [whose] mouth came a sharp double-edged sword" (Rev. 1:16; also 2:12, 16; 19:15).

It must be stressed that the Word has its power because it is the Word of Christ. The Word, in all its keenness, comes out of the mouth of Jesus, who is himself the Word made flesh. The Word is Christ's weapon, and he is the one who wields it. With Trinitarian precision we may also say that the Word that is the sword of Christ is also "the sword of the Spirit," for the Holy Spirit is at work in the Word too.

So also is the Father. Isaiah records God as saying:

> "For my thoughts are not your thoughts,
> neither are your ways my ways,"
>   declares the LORD.
> "As the heavens are higher than the earth,
> so are my ways higher than your ways
> and my thoughts than your thoughts."
>   —Isa. 55:8-9

After thus establishing why human beings need God's Word—how could we know anything about our infinite, transcendent Maker apart from what he reveals to us?—the prophet then underscores the efficacy of the Word, showing that it accomplishes God's purpose because it is living and active:

> "As the rain and the snow
> come down from heaven,
> and do not return to it without
>   watering the earth
> and making it bud and flourish,
> so that it yields seed for the sower and
>   bread for the eater,
> so is my word that goes out from my mouth:
> It will not return to me empty,
> but will accomplish what I desire
> and achieve the purpose for which I sent it."
>   —vv. 10-11

Jesus was undoubtedly alluding to this passage in his parable of the sower who scatters seeds, symbolizing the Word of God (Matt. 13:3-9, 18-23). Granted, as the parable shows, not everyone who hears the Word is changed by it. Some manifest the shallowness of rocky ground; some pay more heed to the thorns of the world. Nevertheless, God's Word never returns to him empty; it always accomplishes his will and achieves his purpose.

Encountering God in the Bible

In what sense do we meet God in the Bible? First, we meet him when we are exposed to his righteousness, when we realize the obedience we owe him, when we know ourselves as sinners in his presence. Second, we meet him when he comes to us as Jesus Christ, offering his grace, mercy, and forgiveness.

God's Law, his instructions for how human beings should live, permeates nearly every page of the Bible. Adam and Eve needed to obey only one easy commandment to live in the garden; Abraham needed to obey God's call; Moses was given the Ten Commandments; the redeemed nation needed to obey elaborate ceremonial and civil statutes; the prophets were sent to condemn personal and social evils.

Jesus not only teaches but models the beauty of God's righteousness. We tend to caricature moral teachings as harsh and unattractive. C. S. Lewis points out how in our literature villains tend to seem much more interesting and believable than the "good guys," who often come across as sappy and unreal. The Bible, however, is a book in which goodness is compelling. And in Jesus Christ we see the one purely good human being, whose compassion, justice, and love are so overwhelming that almost no one, not even unbelievers, calls his character into question.

The point is, the moral content of the Bible is part of God's revelation of himself because he, personally, is a moral being. God's righteousness is manifested not only in his ineffable goodness but in his requirement that we too be righteous.

The Bible and Western Civilization

The moral universe set forth in the Bible has become such a part of our civilization that we take for granted how radical it is, especially in the context of the ancient world. For the Egyptians and the Canaanites (and for tribal societies to this day), there was a continuum between one's gods, nature, and culture. In pagan religions the gods are not particularly righteous at all. Just as nature is not moral, so the gods—being mostly personifications of natural forces, many of them dangerous—are seldom seen as the source of any moral law. Even in advanced pagan cultures such as those of the Greeks and the Romans, the gods of classical mythology are portrayed as amoral, arbitrarily offended, or actually immoral, committing adultery with human women and playing cruel jokes on humanity.

Like nature, culture itself was supposed to be divine, its customs and institutions having their origin in the gods. In ancient Egypt the Pharaoh was understood to be a descendant of a god. The divinity of the king was taken for granted by the Canaanites and even by the sophisticated Romans, who would persecute Christians for refusing to burn incense to the divinized Emperor. To be sure, such societies had their moral beliefs—a reflection of the Law of God inscribed on the hearts even of the Gentiles (Rom. 2:14-15); but they had little conceptual framework for a transcendent law to which even their culture was subject.

According to scholars such as Herbert Schneidau in his book *Sacred Discontent: The Bible and Western Civilization,* the ancient Canaanites—or contemporary pagans in Africa or New Guinea—were and are unable to criticize their leaders. If the king is a god, there is no higher standard by which to judge him. If he commands something unjust, or if the customs of the community mandate some evil, such as the sacrifice of children, there is no conceptual way to question the authority or to change the society. The divinized culture is thus utterly resistant to change, which is why, according to Schneidau, some primitive tribes have remained static for millennia.

In contrast, the Bible teaches that God is transcendent (as opposed to nature deities) and that morality is transcendent. Morality is grounded in the character of the sovereign deity, whose laws are above all individuals and cultures. In the Bible, even the king is accountable to God's moral Law. Thus the prophets come before kings and, bearing God's Word, denounce them for oppressing the widows and orphans and for other acts of personal and social immorality (see 2 Sam. 12, for example).

According to Schneidau, the biblical legacy of a transcendent Law is why the history of the West has been one of constant change. Our institutions and our leaders are not sacred. We can criticize our leaders. We can measure our society by objective moral standards and correct the evils, a never-ending process. This legacy is also the source of our political freedoms. The true radicalism of the biblical worldview will become more and more evident in the future as people continue to revert to the primitive idea that morality is simply a matter of individual values or is merely cultural.

Softening God's Law

Many are trying to soften God's Law in other ways today. People are trying to use the Bible as the ultimate self-help book. Some are trying to abstract principles from its teachings that will supposedly give us happier lives. We are told that if we follow the management principles of Jesus, our businesses will prosper, or that if we follow biblical principles about how we handle money, eat, or conduct our family lives we will be wealthy and healthy, eliminate our problems, and live happily ever after.

To be sure, the Bible is filled with practical wisdom. Many of our problems, such as family dysfunctions, are indeed moral at their root. I am by no means denying that biblical principles reveal much of human nature and the facts of creation and can offer valuable guidance in all spheres of life. If we would or could obey the moral law, we would be much happier and better off. But there is a danger in domesticating God's Law, turning it into an easy-to-follow, step-by-step plan for a problem-free, middle-class lifestyle. This can become problematic in our very view of God and the way we are oriented to him. For God does not exist for us; we exist for him. God is not there primarily to please us; we are here to please him. The notion of a deity who is at our beck and call, who gives good luck in our endeavors if we only follow his prescriptions, is a pagan legacy.

An even more dangerous stance toward God today is our posture of moral superiority to him. The mystery of why a loving God allows so much suffering in the world is a legitimate question, raised in the Bible itself (see Job and Habbakuk). But it is surely the height of insolence for us, in this morally vacuous age, to pass judgment on the source of our very ideas of justice.

Today we have the odd contradiction that people are both blatantly sinful and at the same time self-righteous. Instead of accepting that what they are doing is not right, they insist that their vices are virtues and that no one has the right to criticize their bad behavior. They want to feel good about themselves. They thus react strongly and emotionally against anything that might condemn them. But God's Word is a sword; it cuts deep. The sword of the Spirit hurts, though like a scalpel in the hand of a skilled surgeon, it also heals.

We should never read God's Law in a way that makes us feel complacent. The Law, properly applied, brings us into judgment. It opens our eyes to the extent of our failure to keep it perfectly. It forces us to be honest with ourselves. Before God's Law, we stand condemned.

Our moral sensibility is not enough to accurately assess where we stand. Again, as Isaiah reminds us, "'my thoughts are not your thoughts, neither are your ways my ways,' declares the LORD" (Isa. 55:8). While it is plain that the Levitical laws were intended to set the Hebrew nation apart and are not binding on Gentiles, reading its litany of death penalties—not just for murder and rape but for sexual immorality, disobedience to parents, idolatry, false prophecy, and occultism—gives me the unsettling realization that I too have done things worthy of death. While I might have avoided the worst of the external sins, when I read Christ's Sermon on the Mount my complacency is shattered. For not only murder but anger, not just adultery but sexual fantasies make me subject to God's judgment (Matt. 5:21-22, 27-28). Inner states, no less than external actions, are sinful, and I have little or no control over how I feel inside.

I read that even my acts of righteousness, what little there is of that, are like "filthy rags" before God (Isa. 64:6).

Yet at the very point at which the rigorous demands of God's Law and the impossibility of fulfilling it are at their highest pitch, I read in Romans:

> *But now a righteousness from God, apart from law, has been made known, to which the Law and the Prophets testify. This righteousness*

*from God comes through faith in Jesus Christ
to all who believe. There is no difference, for
all have sinned and fall short of the glory of
God, and are justified freely by his grace
through the redemption that came by Christ
Jesus. God presented him as a sacrifice of
atonement, through faith in his blood.*
—Rom. 3:21-25

Law and Gospel

Thus the Law gives way to the Gospel. There is
another righteousness "apart from law," a righteousness freely given by God, not dependent on
what we do or fail to do at all. We read that the righteousness of Jesus—so complete and compelling—
is imputed to us. Conversely, our sins are imputed
to Jesus, who took their punishment and bore the
curse we deserve. When we are united to Christ in
faith, our sins are covered by the blood Jesus shed
on the cross; and when God looks for our good
works, he sees the works of Jesus.

God's grace is so astoundingly full that the second Person of the Trinity has interceded on our
behalf, assuming our guilt and ascribing to us a
righteousness that is not our own. In this mysteri-
ous transaction, the second Person of the Trinity
took on our flesh and became our sacrifice. He
atoned for our sins. Then he rose again from the
dead, a victory shared by those who are united to
him in faith.

From this side of Christ the Law assumes a different aspect. Someone who is in Christ is no longer
under the Law. There is no more condemnation.
Nevertheless, Christ is at work through his Word,
changing the sinful heart, transforming the inner
life, so that the believer willingly, even sponta-
neously, does what the Law requires after all. Of
course, the process of Christian growth is often

slow and halting and never complete until death, which is why the Christian still needs the Law as a guide for a God-pleasing life and for driving him into a deeper dependence on Christ.

One meets God in the Bible by finding Jesus Christ in its pages. As the passage from Romans points out, this good news of salvation through God's grace is, like the Law, on nearly every page of the Bible. It is not just in the New Testament; rather, it is something to which "the Law and the Prophets testify" (Rom. 3:21).

Christ is prophesied, symbolized, and foreshadowed throughout the Old Testament. No sooner did Adam and Eve fall into sin than God promised that the satanic serpent would be crushed by the seed of the woman. Abraham's son did not have to be sacrificed, because God provided a substitute. (Though God would spare Abraham's son, he would not spare his own.) Abraham needed to have faith in God's promises, as do we. God sent Moses to his enslaved people, delivering them through the blood of the lamb spread upon the doors of their houses. The whole sacrificial system—the tabernacle and temple, the priesthood, the Ark of the Covenant, the bloody altars, the Day of Atonement—all explicate Christ's sacrifice. And so do the many deliverers, the constant patterns of sin, slavery, and rescue, and the prophets delivering the promise of the one who would bear our iniquity.

The Bible is about Christ from cover to cover. The Incarnate Word makes himself known in the written Word.

THREE

The Authority of the Bible

There is no way to know about Christ except from God's Word. Philosophy might speculate abstractly about the existence of God, but philosophical speculation could never dream up the critical notion that God became flesh and died for our sins. Therefore, to know Jesus, his life, works, and personality, one must read the New Testament. To know how God considers us—either as sinful or redeemed—we are utterly dependent on the written revelation.

Reading the Bible is a personal act, as I have tried to show, and God acts on us in a personal way as we read. To read the Bible—including studying it and hearing it preached—is to commune with God. The Holy Spirit is found in the Word. Thus, as we read the Law, the Holy Spirit convicts us of sin; and as we read the Gospel, the Holy Spirit builds faith in our hearts. When we talk with someone we love, we are not just seeking information about him or her. Speaking and listening are ways of being in contact with that person. In the devotional life of the Christian, reading the Bible goes with prayer, both contributing to that mutual communication that constitutes a personal relationship with Jesus Christ.

At the same time, the Bible is also our authority. It must be the sourcebook of our theology. It must be our ultimate touchstone for what is true and false.

Evading God's Word

Human beings have an aversion to God's Law. Being sinful, we do not want to be told what to do. We want to follow our own untrammeled desires; and we certainly do not want to be told there is something wrong with us. But strangely, we also have an aversion to the Gospel—the message of free salvation through the grace of God by means of the sacrifice of Christ. The Gospel stirs an odd hostility among people who insist that they do not need to be saved, or that if they do, they can save themselves. Our fallen nature makes us much more comfortable with man-made religions, domestic gods, and schemes for self-divination. As a result, we have a history of evading God's Word, whether this is in the form of rejecting it altogether, putting some human authority over it, or simply interpreting it away.

1. *Misunderstanding what the Bible is.* Some confusions about the authority of Scripture come merely by misunderstanding what the Word of God is. The Bible consists of a number of separate books. The books of the New Testament were written some years after the time of Christ. The church collected the various books, chose which ones were judged to have apostolic authority, and established the final canon of Holy Scripture. Therefore, it is argued, it was the church that gave the Bible its authority.

But actually the Word preceded the church. Before the Bible was written down, the Word of God existed and was at work. God created the universe through the power of his word, and he spoke his Law and his Gospel through Moses and the prophets, who later wrote them down. The church has its beginnings with Christ, the Word made flesh, who taught his word to his apostles. Moreover, no one can become a Christian apart from hearing words about Jesus. This is because "faith comes from hearing the message, and the message is heard through the word of Christ" (Rom. 10:17).

God's living and active Word was proclaimed by the apostles and evangelists, and the Holy Spirit worked through their words to create faith in the hearts of many who heard it. Later the apostolic testimony was written down, preserved, and collected. The church grew up around the Word, and the public reading of the Word has always been at the heart of Christian worship—to the point that Scripture itself speaks much more of hearing the Word than of reading it.

To this day, God's Word is present wherever and whenever Jesus Christ is proclaimed, be it in a pastor's sermon or in an ordinary Christian's informal witness to a friend. The Holy Spirit is active in those words. Moreover, now that God's Word has been written down, we have an authoritative source that enables us to distinguish between what is in accord with God's Word and what is not. A pastor is preaching God's Word when he is unfolding the text of Scripture, teaching God's Law and the Gospel of Christ—not when he is merely telling a funny story or applying the pop psychology he has found in some magazine. While content like this might legitimately show up in some sermons, those words, strictly speaking, are his and not God's.

The church is subject to God's Word, which called its members to faith and which continues to provide the content of its teaching and the efficacy of its worship and work.

The authority of the Bible derives from its Author, for it is the Holy Spirit who inspired the Bible's human authors, bringing to mind what Christ said ("The Holy Spirit, whom the Father will send in my name, will teach you all things and will remind you of everything I have said to you," John 14:26) and guiding the very words by which they wrote the truth down ("This is what we speak, not in words taught us by human wisdom but in words taught by the Spirit, expressing spiritual truths in spiritual words," 1 Cor. 2:13).

Thus, if the Bible is God's Word, to believe it, obey it, and trust it is to believe, obey, and trust God. Just as the church is subject to Christ, its Head, so is it subject to Christ's Word, in which Christ communicates his truth and will to his people.

2. *The assaults of alleged biblical scholarship.* The major assault on the authority of the Bible has come from certain kinds of biblical scholarship. Beginning with the Age of Reason and continuing through the scientism of the nineteenth and twentieth centuries, certain scholars had the idea of studying the Bible like "any other book." These are just ancient texts, they said. What can be deduced about their history, composition, and original meaning? Studying the ancient contexts can shed light on their meaning, of course, but the approach of these "higher critics" went further.

In essence, by assuming that the Bible is like any other book, these scholars bracketed out any possibility of the supernatural. When they came to a prophecy of an event that clearly occurred in history, such as the fall of Jerusalem, they concluded that since, according to the canons of their scientific scholarship, predictive prophecy cannot take place, the document containing the prophecy must have been written afterwards. They handled the miracles of Jesus in the same way. Since there is no such thing as miracles, they concluded that the Gospel accounts cannot be historical. The Gospels must have been invented by the early church over a long period of "creative" oral tradition.

In other words, the higher critics began by assuming that the Bible is not the Word of God and then constructed alternative explanations that would be credible to nonbelievers. This approach to the Bible has been taught in the seminaries of the mainline, liberal denominations for some time, and it effectively torpedoes the authority of the Bible in those traditions, even though most ministers who were trained to disbelieve the Bible in seminary make a point of keeping what they have learned out of their sermons for fear of scandalizing the people.

3. *The Jesus Seminar.* Recently a group of higher critics has taken the offensive, going public and evangelizing for their cause. They call themselves the Jesus Seminar, and they have been holding press conferences and publishing curriculum for laypeople to disabuse them of the notion that the Bible is the Word of God. In doing so, however, these people have made themselves look ridiculous, even to the secular press. Their scholarly method is for the group of scholars to vote on whether or not a particular part of the Bible actually happened. The spectacle of a bunch of academics solemnly voting on "what Jesus really said" and in the process throwing out almost everything he did say is unintentionally hilarious.

The fact is, even contemporary secular scholars are exploding this kind of methodology. Higher criticism reflects the modernist overconfidence in scientific rationalism, trying to apply it in cases where it cannot possibly apply. The postmodernist scholars, for all their faults, recognize the inherent subjective bias in this supposedly objective approach to the Bible.

They ask, for example, why is it that the feminist members of the Jesus Seminar are willing to accept as authentic only the statements of Jesus that liberate women? Or why is it that the neo-Marxists are willing to keep only the passages in which Jesus criticizes power structures while praising the poor? These selections merely reflect the scholars' own values, so that Jesus is recast in their image. The notion that scholars twenty centuries removed from

New Testament times and from a culture totally alien from the one they are studying can proclaim with dogmatic certainty that they "know" what the ancient texts are actually about is ludicrous.

Yet the spiritual stakes are high. Among the events voted out by the Jesus Seminar is Christ's resurrection from the dead. If the Jesus Seminar and the liberal seminary professors are correct, if the Word of God is merely a human construction, then Christianity is just a big mistake. To belong to a church under such mistaken circumstances is pointless, though the liberal denominations understandably want that practice to continue. In all honesty, if Jesus did not rise from the dead, we should board up the churches, sell them to real estate developers, and sleep in on Sunday mornings. The denial of biblical authority leads quickly to a denial of Christianity.

What higher criticism represents is the larger phenomenon of placing some human authority over the authority of God. When there is a discrepancy between the "scientific" worldview and the Bible, the modernists go with science every time, since for them science has authority over Scripture. When a particular scholarly methodology undermines the claims of the Bible, they do not question the methodology, even though scholarly methodologies come and go. They immediately dismiss the Bible's claims. They consider their method to be what is authoritative. The folly of this is obvious.

4. *Multiple revisions.* Higher criticism has not been the sole manifestation of theological liberalism, which is merely the common impulse to want to change Christianity so that it conforms to a dominant intellectual or cultural trend. During the eighteenth-century Enlightenment, Christianity was revised to conform to the expectations of the Age of Reason. In the nineteenth century Christianity was reworked in terms of romanticized religious feel-

ings. The movements of the twentieth century—existentialism, Marxism, fascism, sixties radicalism, pop psychology, feminism, the New Age movement, and environmentalism—have all had their own truncated and revamped Christianities. It does not seem to matter that such movements change overnight, with one intellectual fad following another, so that Christianity becomes just another revolving door.

One does not have to be a liberal to practice liberal theology either. Churchmen who look to culture rather than to God's Word to determine what they should teach, how they should live, and how they should worship are liberal theologians, even though the culture they are imitating may be conservative.

Human reason—whether in the form of science, philosophy, or informal "common sense"—often functions as an authority to judge and replace Scripture. Thus in our postmodernist era, which assumes that truth is relative, the most common authority is the individual's desires. People "choose" their religious beliefs on the basis of what they "like." They may even accept much of what is in the Bible—the pleasant teachings about heaven and God's love, for instance—but reject what is less likable (such as hell, God's judgment, and the cost of discipleship). Their real authority is their own will, which triumphs over all objective criteria including reason.

The Inerrancy of Scripture

One antidote to these denials of the Bible's authority is confidence in the inerrancy of Scripture, which means that what the Bible teaches is objectively true. As Luther put it in his *Large Catechism* (disproving the notion that this is new teaching), "My neighbor and I—in short, all men—may err and deceive, but God's Word cannot err."

Like all legitimate theological teachings, this one is grounded in what the Bible says about itself. Jesus, the Incarnate Word who is himself "the way and the truth and the life" (John 14:6), acknowledges to his Father that "your word is truth" (John 17:17). That is, not only is God's Word true, it is "truth" itself, the criterion for all other truth-claims.

This does not mean that the Bible is the only thing that is true, that reason and science and experience are not means of knowledge. Nor does it mean that the Bible provides exhaustive knowledge of the objective universe or even of God. The very reason we are in need of God's revelation is that the capacity of the human mind, which is both finite and fallen, is radically limited, especially as regards spiritual matters. Scripture declares, "Now I know in part." Only later, after this mortal life is over, when I will be glorified and face to face with Christ, shall "I . . . know fully, even as I am fully known" (1 Cor. 13:12).

The accumulation of knowledge, for all our great scientific discoveries and scholarly achievements, can never be complete. There will never be a time when we can declare that we know everything, so that the universities and research institutes can all close down. What we discover can be useful. But as the history of science and ideas proves, our discoveries will be subject to constant revision. As new information is uncovered and new issues emerge, new paradigms will be constructed to explain them. The human mind will never run out of things to do.

This is why eternal truths must not be made dependent on the contingent, ever-changing projects of the human intellect. If they are, they can only lose their eternal quality, since human constructions are most emphatically not eternal, as those who construct them will generally admit.

Consider the theory of evolution, for example.

This alleged discovery shook the world of nine-teenth-century Christianity. The Bible says that God created the universe in six days. But Darwin said that species, including human beings, came from chance processes over the course of many millions of years. Science *seemed* to have disproved what the Bible says, and biblical authority was delivered what *seemed* to be a fatal blow.

The conflict is real, of course. The worldview of Darwinism, with its emphasis on random mutations and its exaltation of amoral conflict in the survival of the fittest, is not compatible with the worldview of the Bible, with the Creator and his moral Law. But to abandon the Bible on the tenuous grounds of a scientific theory is to act too hastily.

Set aside the arguments of scientific creationism for a moment, though they have much to commend them. Does anyone imagine that the theory of evolution will exist in its present authoritative form in 700 years? Seven hundred years ago the Ptolemaic model of the universe, with its planetary spheres revolving around a stationary earth, was the paradigm that accounted for the celestial observations of that time and unified the science of that day. Galileo with his more sophisticated astronomical observations called the whole paradigm into question. Christians who had hitched their wagon to the science of the day joined the astrologers in opposing him, but we know now that they only made fools of themselves. Today the theory of evolution is our model, and the new design theory is calling many of its assumptions into question. If the history of science is any guide, Darwin's theory will be replaced by another theory, and that one will also be replaced in time. In the meantime, Christians, however they make use of the scientific knowledge of their age, can rely on the unchanging, eternal truths of God's Word.

It must also be emphasized that we cannot

expect to understand what the Bible teaches in a complete or comprehensive way. Just as we can never find out everything there is to know in nature, so we can never come to the point where we know everything there is to know in the Bible. God's truth is rich, complex, and inexhaustible. We can never study the Bible enough, and we will always discover new insights in its pages.

Interpretation

Another issue in appropriating the authority of Scripture is the vexing problem of interpretation. When the Reformers put the Bible into the hands of nearly all Christians and taught them to read it, the intention was not to make every individual his or her own church. The goal was for each person to meet Christ in a personal way, not for everyone to develop his or her own doctrines. Unfortunately, a great deal of the latter happened, as the plethora of private interpretations and novel theologies that arose in the wake of the Reformation makes evident.

Strictly speaking, interpretation is not the main business of someone who reads the Bible. "Above all," warns Peter, "you must understand that no prophecy of Scripture came about by the prophet's own interpretation. For prophecy never had its origin in the will of man, but men spoke from God as they were carried along by the Holy Spirit" (2 Pet. 1:20-21). The prophets were not "interpreting" God's Word; they were simply speaking as the Spirit carried them along. It would seem to follow that what is most important for readers is the encounter with the Holy Spirit, which does not necessarily require "interpretation."

Sometimes interpretation becomes a pretext for evading what the Bible says. Postmodernists are especially adept at scrutinizing a word so closely that its meaning dissolves. The effect is similar to holding an object so close to your eyes that your eyes no longer focus and the object becomes impossible to see. Thus we have tortuous readings of the Bible to get around its more unpopular teachings. I have read an argument that the Bible does not teach against homosexuality on the ground that scholars do not know what *arsenkoitai* means. However, my own limited study of Greek taught me that *arsen* means "men" and *koitai* means "coitus."

Instead of honestly disbelieving what the Bible says, the effort is often made simply to interpret it away or otherwise twist it to fit one's own predilections. The surest test for one's belief in the authority of the Bible is if someone holds to its teachings even when they are contrary to the person's desires.

Just as the doctrine of the inerrancy of Scripture confronts the modernist critiques of the Bible's objective truth, another ancient doctrine confronts the postmodernist hermeneutical obscurantism—namely, the doctrine of the clarity of Scripture. Though the Bible has some difficult passages, on the whole it is not obscure. What most needs to be communicated—namely, the Law and the Gospel, the message of human sin and God's grace—is as clear as day. As someone has said, "It's not the parts of the Bible that I don't understand that bother me; it's the parts I do understand."

Having said this, the Bible in many ways and at many points does require interpretation. The revelation of an infinite God by its nature must be complex, multifaceted, and challenging to the human mind. So the Bible must not only be read, it must be studied. Scholars who understand the ancient languages, who have researched its contexts and nuances, shed great light on the full meaning of the words. Furthermore, the truths revealed in Scripture must be put together so their full implications can be contemplated as a whole. This is what theology is, the systematization of and reflection upon what the Bible has revealed.

The Analogy of Faith

The Reformers taught something called "the analogy of faith," which means essentially that the Bible interprets itself. The written Word of God, in its comprehensiveness and variety, constitutes a self-contained interpretive system. One part of the Bible interprets another. Obscure passages can be explained in terms of clear passages. Thus the Scriptures must be "examined" (Acts 17:11). We must page back and forth, referencing and cross-referencing to explore the depths of God's entire revelation. Such foundational truths as the Trinity emerge only by assembling the whole range of scriptural teaching, putting together texts that show that the Father is God, that the Son is God, that the Holy Spirit is God and that God is one.

George Herbert put it this way in one of his sonnets:

> *Not only how each verse doth shine,*
> *But all the constellations of the story.*
> *This verse marks that, and*
> *   both do make a motion*
> *Unto a third, that ten leaves off doth lie.*

Yet for Herbert, this Bible study is not so much his interpreting the Bible as it is the Bible interpreting him:

> *Such are thy secrets, which*
> *   my life makes good,*
> *And comments on thee: for in ev'ry thing*
> *Thy words do find me out, and*
> *   parallels bring,*
> *And in another make me understood.*

God's Word outshines the stars both in its light and as a navigational guide, and its message is salvation.

FOUR

Why the Bible
Is Enough

Though a high view of Scripture and submission to the analogy of faith will bring consensus on many of the most important issues, the question remains, how can there be so many different theologies among Bible-believing Christians? There are certain interpretive cruxes—for example, concerning the nature of the sacraments, divine election, and the last days—upon which different groups of believers have disagreed. Lutherans, Calvinists, Baptists, and others all claim to base their theology on the letter of God's Word, yet come to different conclusions.

These constitute what contemporary hermeneutical theorists term "interpretive communities." Though they will debate with each other and occasionally convince someone on the other side, they are pretty much self-contained, constituting a theological tradition, a particular reading of the Bible. They may formulate their beliefs in their formal confessions of faith, but these are not understood to be any kind of additions to Scripture; rather, they are simply the theology they believe Scripture teaches.

Do so many theologies ostensibly based on the Bible mean that the Bible lacks clarity? That it can legitimately mean different things to different people? Not really. It means only that we "know in part," that the Scriptures are greater than all the theologians. Christians must continue to study God's Word and honestly follow where it leads them.

Adding to the Bible

The bigger problem in churches today, including those that claim to hold a high view of Scripture, is the impulse to supplement the Word of God with revelations from other sources. The temptation to rely on human reason, instead of on Scripture alone, has already been discussed. Others rely not only on the Bible but also on personal revelations.

Roman Catholics supplement the Bible with the teaching magisterium of the Church. For those subscribing to biblical teachings recaptured and proclaimed in the Reformation, the church certainly has its teaching ministry; but what is taught is to be drawn from the Word of God. The two must never be at odds with each other (as when a Catholic theologian might say that while the Bible does not teach the Assumption of the Virgin Mary, the Church does, and that is equally authoritative). Roman Catholics believe that the Holy Spirit works in the institution of the Church, so that the Pope, when ruling *ex cathedra*, is infallible. Protestants consider the Bible infallible; Catholics are willing to agree to the authority of the Bible, but they also teach the inerrancy of the pope.

Among Protestants, many evangelicals, including the whole charismatic tradition, believe that the Holy Spirit inspires individuals with supernatural powers and knowledge. They consider themselves to be guided by intuitions, visions, dreams, and inner voices that they take to be from the Holy Spirit himself. They typically believe in the Bible—and use the Scriptures to test these other revelations—but they do not consider the Bible to be sufficient. Rather, it must be supplemented by personal experiences and personal revelations.

Theoretically, if a Christian receives a "word of

knowledge" from the Holy Spirit, that word should have the same status and properties, including inerrancy, as a passage from the Bible.

Luther considered Roman Catholics and those we now call charismatics to be essentially the same. They both, he said, seek to know God apart from his Word. The pope claims direct inspiration from the Holy Spirit. The "enthusiasts" of Luther's day claimed the same privilege for every Christian. The difference, he said wryly, is that the Catholics only have one person who claims this direct inspiration. In the case of the enthusiasts, each person is a pope.

Granting that one meets God in the pages of his Word, we might still ask, is it possible to meet him anywhere else? Certainly the Bible itself teaches that something of God can be deduced from his creation. "For since the creation of the world God's invisible qualities—his eternal power and divine nature—have been clearly seen, being understood from what has been made, so that men are without excuse" (Rom. 1:20). Does this mean there can be a "natural theology" apart from Scripture?

Theological traditions disagree about this, but it is clear in all of them that whatever natural theology there might be, the revelation of God in nature is incapable of saving anyone. The passage in Romans describes a knowledge of God that exists even in the hearts of pagans, a knowledge against which every human being is rebelling, so that everyone, including those who have never heard of the true God, is "without excuse." Saving faith, on the other hand, must come from "hearing" the Word of God (Rom. 10:17).

Or consider the sacraments. What makes them sacraments is the Word of God that is given with the water and with the bread and wine. In answer to the question in the Catechism, "How can water do such great things?" Luther explained his view of baptism by pointing out, "It is not the water indeed that does them, but the Word of God which is in and with the water, and faith, which trusts such Word of God in the water." Luther had a high view of the sacraments, but their power comes from the Word.

What about visions? God revealed himself to the patriarchs, prophets, and New Testament saints directly. Why shouldn't he do the same today? The answer is that before the Word that God gave the patriarchs, prophets, and New Testament saints was written down, he necessarily spoke to them directly. There was no other way. But we do not need that direct address now since we have that Word written in a book.

It has been pointed out that in the book of Acts even those who were given visions did not base their faith on them. Rather, the visionaries were directed to apostles who instructed them by means of the Word. The Roman centurion Cornelius had a vision, but it directed him to Peter, who preached to him the Word of Christ, through which he received the Holy Spirit and was baptized (Acts 10:30-48). Paul on the road to Damascus had a vision of Jesus but still needed the ministry of Ananias to receive his sight, be baptized, and be brought into the church (Acts 9:1-22).

Better Than Visions

In a remarkable passage in his second letter, Peter gives an eyewitness account of the Transfiguration of Jesus Christ.

> We did not follow cleverly invented stories when we told you about the power and coming of our Lord Jesus Christ, but we were eyewitnesses of his majesty. For he received honor and glory from God the Father when the voice came to him from the Majestic Glory, saying, "This is my Son, whom I love; with him I am well pleased." We ourselves heard

> *this voice that came from heaven when we*
> *were with him on the sacred mountain.*
>
> *And we have the word of the prophets*
> *made more certain, and you will do well to pay*
> *attention to it, as to a light shining in a dark*
> *place, until the day dawns and the morning*
> *star rises in your hearts. Above all, you must*
> *understand that no prophecy of Scripture came*
> *about by the prophet's own interpretation. For*
> *prophecy never had its origin in the will of*
> *man, but men spoke from God as they were*
> *carried along by the Holy Spirit.*
>
> —2 Pet. 1:16-21

Here one of the twelve disciples—who traveled with Jesus, heard his teachings, witnessed his miracles, and knew him face to face—exalts the Word of God over his own experience. "We have the word of the prophets made more certain," he says. More certain even than having witnessed the Lord's transfiguration with his own eyes? Yes. For physical vision is at best uncertain, while the Word of God is not. Peter then segues into that great text on the inspiration of the Bible by the Holy Spirit, to which we have referred so many times already.

Or consider what Jesus says in the Gospel of John. Despite all his miraculous deeds, few people believed in Jesus when he was on earth. In fact, even after his resurrection Thomas refused to believe until Jesus appeared to him and insisted that he put his fingers in his wounds. "Because you have seen me, you have believed," said the resurrected Christ. But then he added, referring to us, "Blessed are those who have not seen and yet have believed" (John 20:29).

Put this text together with Christ's high-priestly prayer in which he prayed for his disciples and for us future believers, using the analogy of faith. "I have revealed you to those whom you gave me out of the world. . . . For I gave them the words you gave me and they accepted them" (John 17:6, 8). This means that Jesus, the Incarnate Word, is the authentic revelation of God to his people. Furthermore, the Father gave Jesus "words," which he in turn gave to his disciples. "I have given them your word and the world has hated them, for they are not of the world any more than I am of the world" (v. 14). Then the Lord prays for us, saying, "My prayer is not for them alone. I pray also for those who will believe in me through their message" (v. 20).

Do those who believe through the Word have an advantage over those who knew Jesus face to face? We certainly do. If we were there, watching this unprepossessing Galilean, would we have believed? The Pharisees saw it all but, for the most part, remained skeptical. Many others were impressed by Jesus' healings but abandoned him when they saw he was going to get killed. Even his disciples had little staying power. Would we have done any better? I'm not sure that I would have. I am too conservative and would probably have clung to the certainties of the Pharisees rather than risk the heresy of some new covenant.

But thanks be to God that I have heard his Word, which has revealed to me who Christ is and what he has done for my salvation. Thanks be to God that through his Word the Holy Spirit has created faith in my heart.

FIVE

Feeding on the Word of God

What more could we possibly want than the Word of God? Why would we want to look for him elsewhere than where he has promised to meet us? Do we imagine that we could learn more about God through our own intellects or by delving into ourselves? Do we think that the techniques we dream up—for evangelizing, worshiping, solving our problems, or running our lives—will be more powerful than the Bible? We underestimate the magnitude of what God has given us in the Bible. We have God's Word on our bookshelves. We can hold it in our hands. We can access his self-revelation anytime we want.

I have been referring to the act of reading God's Word, but I need to add here that this takes place not merely as part of one's private devotions but also in the church. Here God's Word is read together by his people; it is studied, and it is preached.

Christian worship consists largely of God's Word. The great hymns and liturgies derive directly from it. The Psalms and the responses, the prayers and the Scripture readings immerse the worshipers in the Word of God and therefore bring the worshipers into his presence. In the sermon the pastor proclaims not just his word but the Word of God. A good sermon plunges us into the depths of

Scripture, opening up the text, explaining and applying what God has said. A good sermon will cut us to the quick with the Law and heal us with the balm of the Gospel.

The phenomenon of preaching makes clear another quality of Scripture. It is inexhaustible. A good expositor can open up levels upon levels of insight from a single verse. The rewards of close Bible study—not the kind where everyone just shares his or her feelings about a passage, but the kind that delves deep into the text—are unfathomable. "Open my eyes," says the psalmist in the great paean to the riches of God's Word, "that I may see wonderful things in your law" (Ps. 119:18).

The Bible is something to feed on. Jesus battled the devil with words of Scripture when he was tempted in the wilderness, and when the devil suggested that Jesus perform a miracle to break his fast, our Lord responded with a text from Deuteronomy: "It is written: 'Man does not live on bread alone, but on every word that comes from the mouth of God'" (Matt. 4:4; Deut. 8:3).

The nourishment of Scripture keeps us in the true faith, bringing us again and again to repentance, forgiveness, obedience, and closeness to God. Hearing the preaching of God's Word, studying Scripture with other believers, and reading the Bible on one's own keep the Christian alive as surely as physical food is necessary for physical survival.

We live in a time of spiritual starvation. People own Bibles and even claim to believe in them, but Bible reading and Bible literacy are at all-time lows. Many churches have stopped, or radically cut back, the reading of the Scriptures in their services to make more time for pop music. Pastors are preaching from their own creative imaginations rather than preaching God's Word. To be sure, quite a few churches are growing, attracting numbers through the application of sociological principles and marketing devices. But they are trying to live by bread alone, and not on every word that comes from the mouth of God.

I began by describing my experience of reading the Bible for the first time and how I came face to face with my own sin and the grace of God. Ever since I have kept reading. Reading three chapters a day will take you through the entire Bible in about a year. Reading only one chapter a day will take you on a spiritual pilgrimage that takes three years. Another good scheme I have found is to read a chapter of the Old Testament and a chapter of the New, plus a Psalm, reading through the sequence over and over.

Bad habits are hard to break, and so are good habits. Now I cannot go to sleep until I have done my reading. The "begats" of the genealogies, the repeated instructions on how to build tabernacles and temples, the exhaustive prescriptions for ceremonies and sacrifices that are no longer required— I admit these are tedious, but I have come to love them too. God has written down so many names, showing how he values individuals and their contributions to the unfolding of his plan, reminding me of the names God has written in his Book of Life. The architectural plans, so exactly commanded, remind me that God cares how things are built—after all, he built the universe—and that he honors human craftsmanship. The detailed ceremonial regulations remind me that God cares how he is worshiped, that he demands the beauty of holiness, and that no one can come into his presence without the blood of the Lamb.

But as I read chapter by chapter, year in and year out, I am struck by the way, in the words of Herbert's poem, "thy words do find me out." God's Word has been like a commentary on my own life. When I have had problems, my Bible reading—

sometimes in startling ways—has addressed them. When I needed to be knocked down, God's Law brought me to my knees. When I needed to be built up, the promises of the Gospel were just what I needed to hear. Through deaths of loved ones, professional trials, family worries, and sheer melancholy for no particular reason, I have found inexpressible comfort in God's Word. And in my times of happiness, which are far more frequent, I am also brought to my knees in gratitude for God's inexplicable grace.

Herbert describes Holy Scripture as a mirror "that mends the looker's eyes," meaning that the Bible helps us to see ourselves clearly, as we really are before God, while also, as a means of grace, changing us into what we should be.

Some charge those who love the Bible so much with "bibliolatry," with worshiping a book. We are, of course, not worshiping a book, but the One who wrote it. Nevertheless, I sometimes come close to accepting the charge, such is the access to himself God gives us in the Bible, so real and intimate is his connection to his Word. Many people assume the Word is small and insignificant, of little account compared to some spectacular religious experience or display of earthly power. But we remember that Jesus came not in glory but as a poor baby cradled in a manger, one who would grow up to die on a cross, and thus remember too that God's ways are not our ways.

That God reveals himself in a book may seem too simple, too unspiritual, not mystical enough. One might excuse someone for thinking it too good to be true. But it is true. The God who became man has revealed himself in human language. And his Word, recorded in a book, is the power of salvation.

FOR FURTHER
READING

Boice, James Montgomery. *Standing on the Rock: Biblical Authority in a Secular Age,* revised edition. Grand Rapids, Mich.: Baker, 1994.

Bruce, F. F. *The New Testament Documents: Are They Reliable?* Downers Grove, Ill.: InterVarsity Press, 1974.

Kistler, Don, editor. *Sola Scriptura: The Protestant Position on the Bible.* Morgan, Pa.: Soli Deo Gloria Publications, 1995.

Packer, J. I. *"Fundamentalism" and the Word of God.* Grand Rapids, Mich.: Eerdmans, 1958.

—. *God Has Spoken.* Downers Grove, Ill.: InterVarsity Press, 1979.

Preus, Robert. *The Inspiration of Scripture.* Edinburgh: Oliver & Boyd, 1957.

Saucy, Robert L. *The Bible: Breathed from God.* Wheaton, Ill.: Victor Books/SP Publications, 1978.

Schaeffer, Francis A. *No Final Conflict: The Bible Without Error in All That It Affirms.* Downers Grove, Ill.: InterVarsity Press, 1975.

Sproul, R. C. *Knowing Scripture.* Downers Grove, Ill.: InterVarsity Press, 1977.

Warfield, Benjamin Breckinridge. *The Inspiration and Authority of the Bible,* ed. Samuel G. Craig. Philadelphia: Presbyterian and Reformed, 1948.

Wenham, John. *Christ and the Bible.* Grand Rapids, Mich.: Baker, 1994.